Lean Banking

By Ade Asefeso MCIPS MBA

Copyright 2014 by Ade Asefeso MCIPS MBA
All rights reserved.

First Edition

ISBN-13: 978-1502509420

ISBN-10: 1502509423

Publisher: AA Global Sourcing Ltd
Website: http://www.aaglobalsourcing.com

Table of Contents

Disclaimer 5
Dedication 6
Chapter 1: Introduction 7
Chapter 2: Next Frontiers for Lean 11
Chapter 3: Lean in Banking Sector 13
Chapter 4: The Importance of Engaging Frontline Employees 17
Chapter 5: Lean Approach Should Differ by Industry 19
Chapter 6: Applying Lean Principles in Banking .. 23
Chapter 7: Getting Lean for the Lean Times Ahead 29
Chapter 8: Managing Cost 37
Chapter 9: The Principle of Lean Banking 41
Chapter 10: Using Cause and Effect Diagram 45
Chapter 11: Leveraging Lean in Banking Sector ... 49
Chapter 12: Using Lean in Wholesale Banking 55
Chapter 13: Cutting Costs While Reducing Risks . 65
Chapter 14: Application of Lean to Financial Services 75
Chapter 15: Implementing Lean in a Banking Sector 79
Chapter 16: Incremental Implementation 89
Chapter 17: Lean Approach to Big Data 91
Chapter 18: Making Lean Work 97
Chapter 19: Lean Banking Success Stories 103

Chapter 20: Bank Turns to Lean 107
Chapter 21: Conclusion 115

Disclaimer

This publication is designed to provide competent and reliable information regarding the subject matter covered. However, it is sold with the understanding that the author and publisher are not engaged in rendering professional advice. The authors and publishers specifically disclaim any liability that is incurred from the use or application of contents of this book.

If you purchased this book without a cover you should be aware that this book may have been stolen property and reported as "unsold and destroyed" to the publisher. In this case neither the author nor the publisher has received any payment for this "stripped book."

Dedication

To my family and friends who seems to have been sent here to teach me something about who I am supposed to be. They have nurtured me, challenged me, and even opposed me.... But at every juncture has taught me!

This book is dedicated to my lovely boys, Thomas, Michael and Karl. Teaching them to manage their finance will give them the lives they deserve. They have taught me more about life, presence, and energy management than anything I have done in my life.

Chapter 1: Introduction

Lower costs and additional revenue prove that modern efficiency programs that have long been standard in other industries are now having an effect in the banking sector as well.

Commercial banks should adopt lean principles to ensure long-term sustainability since customers demand quick and efficient services in a competitive environment which only lean institutions could provide by increasing efficiencies and reducing costs.

Lean is both an attitude and an administration philosophy, which can change key areas of banking operating model. Lean helps redefine procedures, composition, purpose, and organisation, it improves relationship with partners and end customers. Lean principles are part of everyday life of a successful organisations.

A successful lean program will results in improved customer services, reducing cycle times by up to 50 percent. The capacity to deliver is enhanced by more than 35 percent, control of operational risk is highly enhanced. Decision making is improved and constant learning process ensured due to lean culture mindset.

Banks should set aggressive targets for improving customer experience, motivating employee engagement, and achieving solid economic payback. Lean management should go beyond process improvement and aim changes in operating model components, such as footprint, organisational design, and IT architecture.

It is not advisable to try to make the entire bank lean in one go, it is better to begin with few pilot projects to educate the core lean implementation team about the lean concept. The implication of the lean processes on efficiency and viability of the project is assessed before expanding it at wider scale in the organisation.

We suggest that you do not set unrealistic targets as failure at pilot stage would undermine the entire lean management plan before it is launched at broader level.

Lean management principles should be applied at the pilot stage. Highest priority should be given to payment operations, like item processing, lock box, vault and wire. Print statements and mail, online on-boarding and servicing, consumer collection and recovery and mortgage collection and recovery operations should be given top priority in lean management regime.

As far as fraud and loss prevention operations are concerned, lean management should be the lowest priority. You cannot take undue risk by going lean in such cases, non-fraud disputes and commercial treasury operations also come under low priority in lean management. Credit card operations (including decision making and complaint handling) and special lending to students, small businesses and traders should also fall under low priority.

Success of lean program depends on correct and efficient execution of pilot project findings. Banking sector should have clear understanding of the targeted objectives of the lean program. Transparency is essential for achieving the goals set in the program; with unclear procedures and non-transparent goals different teams within the organisation would produce inconsistent and conflicting results. This may move the bank in the wrong direction. Most of these banks will find themselves disappointed, because few lean initiatives, in our experience, deliver the expected results. The near and longer-term impact on costs proves to be far less than expected, and any gains in efficiency prove to be either temporary or too limited in scope to make a real difference. There is no fundamental, lasting change in the way the bank conducts its operations and hence little impact on long-term performance.

The problem is not with lean itself however; indeed, we believe that lean has much to offer banks. The problem lies in the approach and implementation. Typically, banks go wrong in one of two ways. One, they apply lean too narrowly and from too limited a perspective. There is no cohesive, end-to-end view of the process itself or the alignment of all of its elements. Alternatively, the effort is driven solely from the top down and fails to engage and involve the key people who actually perform the critical tasks within the process. This leads to a lack of process ownership and accountability. The end result, in either case, is that the lean effort delivers only a fraction of its potential benefits.

In this book, we will discuss what we consider to be the optimal means of deploying lean in the banking sector. Specifically, we advocate a holistic lean program that addresses underlying processes and employee behaviours and attitudes. We also recommend an incremental, pilot-based approach to adoption, one that allows banks to generate quick wins and establish a culture of continuous self-improvement. These elements, we believe, can mean the difference between an unsuccessful lean initiative and a truly transformational one.

Chapter 2: Next Frontiers for Lean

Lean has transformed how leading companies think about operations; starting in assembly plants and other factory settings and moving more recently into services ranging from retailing and health care to banking, IT, and even the public sector. Yet despite lean's trajectory, broad influence, and level of general familiarity among senior executives, it would be a mistake to think that it has reached its full potential.

Indeed, we believe that as senior executives gain more exposure to lean and deepen their understanding of its principles and disciplines, they will seek to drive even more value from it. The opportunities available to them are considerable. For example, powerful new data sources are becoming available, along with analytical tools that make ever more sophisticated frontline problem solving possible. Similarly, leading-edge companies are discovering that lean can supply strong insights about the next frontiers of energy efficiency. Toyota itself is pushing the boundaries of lean, rethinking the art of the possible in production-line changeovers, for example, and bringing customer input more directly into factories and leading service-based companies such as banks are extending the value of lean further still, into areas beyond manufacturing.

What is more, new technologies, new analytical tools, and new ways of looking at customers are making it possible, with greater precision than ever before, to learn what they truly value. The implications are profound because one of the primary constraints on the ability to design a perfect lean system in any operating environment has always been the challenge of understanding customer value.

When lean met banking

The present round of improvements won't be the first time lean has catalyzed management innovation by bringing together what seemed to be strange bedfellows. The first time around, lean operating principles were applied to service industries that had not previously thought of themselves as having factory-like characteristics.

Since retail banking involves a physical process not unlike an assembly line, the handling of paper checks and credit-card slips lends itself readily to lean-manufacturing techniques and their impact can be dramatic; the faster a bank moves cheques through its system, the sooner it can collect its funds and the better its returns on invested capital.

Chapter 3: Lean in Banking Sector

Lean offers banks many advantages. It can effectively address anywhere from 25 to 30 percent of a retail bank's cost base and is a particularly potent tool for lowering front-office and operations costs. Gains in process cycle times can be even more dramatic, with improvements of 30 to 60 percent possible. Improved operational controls, reduced risk, fewer errors, and greater speed lead, in turn, to improved customer experiences and satisfaction.

Lean's benefits go even further. Lean-based thinking can help management understand what customers value most and where it makes the most sense to focus improvements in operations and service levels. Improved organizational engagement via lean particularly among the frontline staff can lead to increased moral and reduced attrition and a successful lean-transformation effort can instil a firm-wide mindset of self-reliance and continuous improvement, one that keeps performance on an upward trajectory.

The challenge lies in the application. Lean needs to be applied holistically that is, from an organization-wide, cross-functional perspective. Targeting only individual "silos" will doom the effort to failure. Lean also needs to be supported by true cultural change, from the top of the organization to the bottom. The senior leadership team must believe in and demonstrate commitment to the effort, and middle managers and frontline workers must feel engaged and be empowered to contribute. Lean thinking and a culture of continuously raising the bar on performance must permeate the organization's psyche and become part of its DNA and its performance-management system.

To facilitate this process, lean must be phased in incrementally rather than through a "big bang" approach. A series of well-targeted and well-sequenced pilot programs, whereby success breeds success, will lay the groundwork for the necessary organizational and cultural changes to "stick" and for lean's benefits to last.

A Holistic Approach

A holistic, multifaceted approach to a lean initiative will incorporate top-down, bottom-up, and "middle-out" components. The top-down component consists of identifying clear goals; focusing on processes that tie directly to competitive advantage and value creation; taking a cross-functional, end-to-end view that starts with the customer and works backward; and securing executive commitment. The bottom-up component consists of engaging frontline workers and managers and empowering them to own and drive process improvement, not just once but on an ongoing basis. The middle-out component is the empowerment of middle managers to apply checks and balances to frontline-driven change recommendations and implement change across the organization. Collectively, these measures lay the groundwork for fundamental and self-sustaining process improvement.

How might this work in practice?

Let's look at the mortgage-application process. This is a process that, in most banks, is plagued by a multitude of inefficiencies, including long cycle times from application to approval, numerous handoffs throughout the process, and the involvement of too many functional silos, often leading to a poor customer experience. To optimize this process via lean, a bank would start with the things that are most important to the customer, such as access to the mortgage application form through multiple channels, clear presentation of and directions for completing all necessary documentation, ease of data entry and immediate identification of entry errors, and a rapid approval process. Working backward through the process chain, the bank would examine the specifics of the process for example, the roles of those involved, the performance metrics, and the mechanics of the handoffs from start to finish. It would apply lean principles to optimize performance for example, to minimize or eliminate paper flow throughout the process, optimize data entry and error-proofing, and ensure that automation is used where logistically and economically feasible. Managers and, in particular, frontline staff would be actively engaged throughout this effort and would continue to try to identify areas where the process might be improved and streamlined.

The underlying philosophy a continuous focus on customers, value drivers, and cost optimization accompanied by supportive changes to organizational behaviours and attitudes are what allow the lean program to deliver its transformational effects. Improvement spans multiple functions, is sustainable, and lays a foundation for additional, broader improvement across the organization.

Development of Organizational Alignment

The organizational alignment achieved via the three pronged approach is a key enabler of lean. Senior management, middle management, and frontline personnel become of one mind regarding the vision and objectives of the transformation and play their respective roles in making it a success. Senior management provides visible leadership and commitment to the effort and communicates that commitment consistently and strategically. Frontline staff members work actively to identify solutions and improve results. Middle management vets the frontline staff's solutions and assures stakeholders that any recommendations being implemented are sound and both middle and senior management confirm that changes are being made across business and functional units.

Chapter 4: The Importance of Engaging Frontline Employees

A closely related element, and one to which most banks give short shrift when trying to implement lean, is change management. Effective change-management practices can identify and address behavioural and organizational issues that hamper process efficiency. This capability is particularly vital for lean initiatives, which require banks to engage workers in unfamiliar ways for example, empowering and encouraging frontline workers to actively challenge the status quo and work on problem solving. Change management can also establish momentum for supportive cultural change by instilling mindsets and behaviours that encourage continuous learning and self-improvement.

In fact, we consider change management to be as important as the "hard" work behind process optimization and we believe it should be actively managed from day one. Some managers might view this as a hindrance, but ultimately it can simplify their task and improve the eventual outcome. Experience shows that employees are more likely to resist new approaches when they don't understand their role and how they can contribute. It is vital to remove such stumbling blocks so that the staff is fully engaged and committed.

Frontline employees; those closest to the process typically have many ideas that can improve process efficiency and add value; but those ideas are often not aired, either because there is no forum for sharing them or because the employees feel undervalued and hence are reluctant to speak out. The end result is that the bank fails to leverage what could be a key competitive weapon.

A properly implemented lean program places a heavy emphasis on engaging these employees and actively tapping into their insights and expertise. This delivers a range of benefits. The most immediate is that process efficiency does, indeed, improve. Employees are also considerably more willing to buy into a new approach or program, because they now feel that they are a valued and vital part of the process.

The advantages go further. They include greater job satisfaction, increased opportunities for training and career development, and lower attrition owing to the reduction of busywork. The benefits of lower attrition, in particular, cannot be overstated. Most banks lose from 15 to 25 percent of their frontline employees and first-line managers in operational areas annually. Hence, there is always a large percentage of the staff that are learning how to do thier job. Shaving this percentage by even a few points via lowered attrition can have a significant impact on productivity.

Chapter 5: Lean Approach Should Differ by Industry

"Let the process flow." "Let the customer pull." This is what is written in manufacturing books about making processes Lean. But it is not always that simple.

Consider this banking example. A customer arrives at a bank branch. He enters, is welcomed by an employee and offered a cup of coffee. He explains his interest in obtaining a loan and a salesperson asks the right questions to identify his exact needs. They enter a lot of data into the bank's computer systems. The data is evaluated at a central clearing point where a decision is made to approve the loan, and the customer gets the money.

On the surface, this seems like a Lean process. There is flow in the process, no batching and the customer pulls (nobody gives him advice, or a loan, unless he comes into the bank or otherwise expresses his interest). But is the process Lean?

Actually, in most cases it is far from Lean given these factors
1. The double entry into different systems that were not linked.
2. Many data points that were not really needed.
3. A lot of waste because decision making had to be taken to the central underwriters.

There are many projects where Lean is not about flow and pull, but about straightforward waste reduction.
Most of the waste is relatively easy to find but hard to eliminate from an information technology-driven process. The key is to make Lean thinking (and usability) a key building block of the design and the review of IT applications.

A successful Lean approach needs to be designed for the industry in which it is supposed to deliver results. It is not enough to adapt the manufacturing experience and it is certainly not enough to use a reduced manufacturing toolkit. Lean banking includes elements that Lean manufacturing gurus have never thought of.

One of the challenges in banking and financial services is that processes often are not easily seen because they are hidden in workflow systems, phone calls and emails. There is no production line to follow with a "walk the process" as a first step in trying to find waste; but the further apart process steps are from each other, the more important and eye-opening a walk the process becomes. Sometimes people up and down the process have never even talked to each other before.

At a bank, the back office was carrying a significant backlog and the decision was made to use Lean to improve the situation. Of course, it was useful to do 5S (an approach to ensure having "a place for everything and everything in its place") and to eliminate some non-value-added steps. When selling loans over the phone, there is no batching either and a transaction is only initiated once the customer says go. No job for the introduction of flow and pull however, while the front office was selling extremely well, it too was overloaded at times. The answer was level loading, or smoothing the demand curve to avoid extreme peaks and deep valleys leading to a better capacity management. Generally, idle time for staff is an important area for waste in services and transactions.

Mistake Proofing as a Lean Solution

Customers are regularly required to fill out insurance claim forms, loan applications or other documents. Unfortunately these documents too often are incomplete or incorrectly filled out. This can be a big problem and a challenge for Lean. That also is true of customers who move without providing their new address. A great deal of waste is generated and sales volumes are reduced when applications are not completed, and extra resources must be expended to fill the missing gaps or correct the errors.

Mistake proofing (designing errors out of the process using simple solutions) is the most promising Lean answer to these problems, and it can be implemented relatively easily in electronic application processes. In many situations, simplifying requirements is the key to success. The less asked of the customer, the less the chance the customer will make an error or forget something, or be frustrated by their own mistake. Sometimes mistake proofing is not required; the bank need only explain why it needs the information in question.

Flow also is difficult to implement if the bank must wait for the customer to react. Take a collections process for example. The agent calls, the customer pays (or does not pay), the agent calls again, the customers pays, and often stops paying again. In this case, the bank was able to improve the performance without even thinking about flow. The solution was to standardize the process, the decisions and their consequences. Giving call agents clear guidelines and simplifying a process for them and the customer can make collecting the outstanding money more effective while keeping customers away from the hassle and costs of legal actions.

Of course, flow makes great sense for longer banking processes, such as mortgage applications. There are many successful examples of this however, for shorter processes or ones that do not need attention to flow and pull, Lean can still be successfully applied.

Chapter 6: Applying Lean Principles in Banking

In the aftermath of the financial crisis, banks have been looking to reduce their cost-to-income ratios by radically improving their operational model in order to continue the deleveraging process and build capital buffers as required by financial regulators. With that goal in mind, cost reduction initiatives have been launched across the entire banking industry.

Department budgets have been slashed, back-offices are being relocated and jobs have been shed worldwide, notably in investment banking. In the meanwhile, banks face more demanding customers, competition of new low-cost players and lower customer loyalty. In a nutshell, banks have to deliver high quality customized customer service across different channels while raising operational efficiency to reduce costs. To tackle these two major operational challenges, more and more banks are turning to operational excellence projects inspired by the Lean methodology.

Aligning processes to customer demands through end-to-end ownership.

Traditionally, banks were organized in a product-centred logic with products being pushed towards the market rather than pulled by customers. With business units organized around products, every change in business or market requirements resulted in department-specific initiatives, creating functional silos. Today, banks are shifting to a customer-centred logic where processes that are valued by the customer, like a credit card or mortgage credit application, are managed in an end-to-end way. The result should be an organization where processes are managed from the moment where the customer expresses his demand until the product or service delivery to the customer.

To manage end-to-end processes in the most effective way, process owners need to be identified to ensure efficient cross-functional collaboration and decision making by bridging the gaps between different departments. The process owner is responsible for managing and improving the entire end-to-end process. To empower the process owner he or she needs to be held accountable through process performance related objectives.

As this type of organization is quite a radical change to the ingrained culture of most banks, resistance is often met at the level of functional managers who fear losing power to the process owners. It is therefore crucial to clearly define roles and responsibilities, e.g. through the RACI (Responsible, Accountable, Consulted, Informed) framework. Developing a process ownership framework is a lengthy task; therefore management must be involved early. A senior management board, consisting of process sponsors should be established. They provide the budget and use their authority to take decision when conflicts arise in one or more end-to-end processes. The process owners report directly to the board.

The identification of process owners themselves, is obviously also key in the success of this approach. It is preferable that the process owner already has some clout within the organization, he will also need a differentiated set of skills; business knowledge, functional expertise and client orientation. It is therefore important to incorporate Human Resources representatives early on to ensure that the best qualified individuals execute this role.

Raising efficiency by applying lean techniques to banking operations.

There is often scepticism whether Lean, which originated in the manufacturing world, applies to the financial services industries. As banks are very process-intensive with complex flows of information across the business, Lean offers an enormous potential for operational improvement by eliminating process wastes. Rework due to errors in the process, unnecessary verification points, physical dispersion of information, process loopbacks, multiple storage of information, delivering services the clients doesn't need,… the list of wastes is quite long. By eliminating these wastes more time can be spent on process steps that create value for the customer. Based on this approach, most banks have started lean initiatives to improve the performance of operations.

It is yet unclear to which extent other Lean concepts and tools are used business-wide to assess the performance of operations and to empower employees in improving them. The Value Stream Map, for example, is a very strong tool to map the end-to-end processes and tie them to different metrics like cycle time (time per task), lead time (process time; e.g. "time between loan application and approval"). These metrics are best used as KPIs by the process owner to assess the end-to-end performance of their respective processes; but these metrics should also be made visible to the process workers, as they must understand their role in the process and how they can play a part in its continuous improvement.

As risk is a core function of the bank, it cannot be neglected during the lean transformation. While processes are optimized to run more efficiently, quality control and risk management must improve along. While Lean in banking is often focused on back-office operations, it can be especially successful at mitigating operational risk when implemented in front-offices by standardizing processes and empowering front-line employees.

Creating a Lean culture and ensuring continuous improvement

Lean is mostly perceived and executed as a methodology to improve operations while the cultural aspects of Lean are often forgotten. It is therefore that very few companies can be actually called "Lean Enterprises". The essence of the Lean culture is that every employee, on every level, tries to improve his work environment and methods from day-to-day.

Often, a project team will lead the lean initiative and will develop a planned approach to raise performance to a certain target. As the project terminates, there is no insurance that the improvement initiatives will continue and old habits will rapidly come back to life.

Communication is the most important step in change management. A bank needs to share a common goal and set of expectations of value that the lean program will deliver. Teaching and coaching Lean techniques to employees is a needed investment to sustain the Lean culture. The concept of the "internal client" should also be introduced for non-customer-facing departments. This approach will ensure a customer-centred attitude at every level of the bank. Finally, Lean managers must spend more time on the floor to observe and capture improvement ideas.

The focus of Lean lies on building a client-centred organization. Banks have always struggled to deliver excellent customer experience due to processes that are not adapted to the customer's need. Moreover, it is mostly a negative perception of the banking industry that hurts customer satisfaction. Lean initiatives are rising rapidly in banking, yet their approach is still too much focused on reaching operational excellence. A focus on the cultural aspects of Lean would ensure, in the first place, that the entire organization is working together in improving its customer service, but more importantly, all employees will be inspired to deliver continuously excellent customer service.

Chapter 7: Getting Lean for the Lean Times Ahead

In light of recent economic, regulatory, financial and social pressures, there is an unprecedented demand on financial service organisations to make best use of the critical resources they have to deliver greater levels of service at the lowest possible cost. Companies have never been more dependent on their staff to deal with the significant level of change and uncertainty that currently exists, yet staff engagement levels in the industry are low. These challenges can and are typically addressed separately; however, if implemented the right way, Lean can simultaneously address all three issues of service, cost and staff engagement; the 'triple play' solution.

Lean has been implemented within Financial Services companies for a number of years, however now is the time to ensure that it is being used to its full effect to achieve its triple play benefits.

Toyota pioneered the use of Lean methods that continue to deliver significant cost reductions, improved staff moral and superior customer service in manufacturing industries, world-wide. The triple play effect of Lean Manufacturing has enabled many organisations to create a significant competitive advantage. Lean is proven to deliver up to a 30% reduction in costs and increase customer satisfaction and staff engagement by 50%.

Below are simple and engaging approach to sustainably introduce, scale and embed Lean methods within Financial Services using four key steps:
1. Understand the voice of the customer.
2. Design the operation around the needs of the customer.
3. Implement the Lean changes.
4. Drive continuous improvement.

1. Understand the voice of the customer.

"Customer centricity" is often used to describe an organisation's service strategy however supporting processes, governance and behaviours fail to genuinely align to this strategic intent. In most cases, the internal organisation structure determines the process rather than the customer needs, and as such many activities fail to add value to the customer at all.

Best practice firms design their organisations around what the internal or external customer values together with the customer journey. Using customer surveys and analysing consumer buying behaviours and patterns, organisations can understand what clients value and what they don't. They can identify the key value streams or activities to deliver the relevant services to the customer. When the value streams have been identified, organisations can use the customer data to identify the high value activities which they need to perfect and the low value activities that must be made more efficient or indeed eliminated altogether.

We worked with a credit card provider to review and value the key needs of their customers. Three of the seven major steps in the customer journey were determined to be high value for the customer. Twenty sub-processes in these high priority areas were not delivering against the stated customer promises as the processes took many more days than advertised. The client used Lean techniques to review these identified high value processes to streamline the activities. As a result of removing waste, processes increased in speed (some cases were 50% faster) improving customer experience. In addition, not only was the customer experience improved but costs were reduced, as certain low value processes were eliminated a true win-win solution.

2. Design the operation around the needs of the customer.

In many financial services organisations, when a standard new account application form is processed there are often multiple handoffs as the paper moves from the front to back office. Each team in the process understands and improves its specific part in the process but staff are rarely given the opportunity to review the end to end process. Due to the limitations of not seeing the full value stream, significant customer and efficiency opportunities fail to be unlocked.

Once the most important customer value streams have been identified, our experience has shown that best practice financial service organisations map and design the value stream from the first customer touch point right through to the final delivery. Mapping the highest value activities from start to finish also shapes the organisational and governance model. New governance structures are required that create a single point of accountability for each end-to-end value stream. In addition, broad staff involvement is key to accurately map the full end-to-end process. Frontline staff involvement is especially important at this stage as they are closest to the process issues, understand the root causes and have the most pragmatic solutions.

Recent Example.

The back office payments function at a large bank were taking 50% longer to process customer payments than the industry benchmark. Using the Lean thinking process, a cross-functional team mapped the end-to-end process. This identified that the branches were failing to complete or check payment request forms correctly resulting in a significant amount of extra work for the back office team. A new approach was designed whereby the front and back office team communicated continuously and regularly met to review quality performance across the process and collectively owned a plan of continuous improvement. As a result, processing costs were halved and the cycle time improved by 100%. In addition, levels of staff frustration were significantly reduced as they were involved in solving a problem they had to deal with for years and as a result eliminated a extremely painful process.

3. Implement the Lean changes

Implementing Lean changes across a value chain that has historically been managed in functional silos is a significant challenge. Functional leaders may feel a loss of control and unclear when working within an environment with a functional manager as well as an end-to-end process manager. Functional managers will have contrasting objectives to the process owners, restricting progress in improving the processes. This complexity increases when addressing multiple processes being followed across several geographies and regulatory jurisdictions. This is a major reason why many organisations struggle to get the traction required to reap the full benefits of Lean as it requires a deep cultural change in addition to a change to processes, systems and structures. Lean thinking must therefore start from the top, with the leadership team.

Our experience illustrates that Leadership support is vital at this stage to ensuring the business overcomes these highly political and cultural barriers. Leaders need to help their teams understand the benefits of collaborating and focusing on customer value and where required be prepared to change the accountabilities and incentives of their leaders to align them to the customer drivers. In addition, successful implementations of Lean have been completed using an incremental, test and lean approach rather than a big bang approach.

All too frequently organisations think that Lean is a simple set of tools and techniques that can be deployed by training courses alone. This fails to understand and address the more important cultural and behavioural change required. Many organisations also find particular success in sustaining Lean efforts by piloting, tailoring and proving the approach in a few select areas first, before rolling it out across their full operation. Having the ability to prove the benefit of Lean in one area of the business helps create buy-in for other parts of the business to adopt it. Once piloted, best practices and a standardised approach can be designed resulting in the creation of a robust, phased Lean implementation plan.

We recently worked with a large international bank who's previous attempts at implementing Lean had been successful within business units but failed to get traction with processes that cut across business unit boundaries. It was identified that the individual business unit managers' performance targets conflicted with the Lean process targets. The senior leadership team had not agreed how they would work together in these cross-business situations. Individually, leaders felt they were sacrificing their own performance due to Lean. One senior leader stated "it feels like they are blaming my team for the problems occurring further downstream". In response senior leaders and managers were taken through a series of Lean simulation and coaching events. This provided the team, within a compressed one-day timeframe, with an illustration of how their decisions and behaviours could help or hinder operational performance. They recognised immediately that short term and siloed decision making would improve their own performance but impact the overall process efficiency. As a result, the governance structure and targets were changed at senior leadership level, aligning them to the specific value stream. The business units agreed to appoint a single owner of the value stream who was accountable for the overall end-to-end process and service level agreements. Their job was to work with the individual business units to improve process performance. With greater transparency of performance, over a six month period, the overall process was made 20% more efficient and took 10% less time to complete.

Chapter 8: Managing Cost

Financial service businesses have cut costs dramatically over the past few years however, meeting profit expectations is still a challenge. For some businesses, meeting profit expectations at current, lower levels of business is proving to be a major headache. In other cases, business and revenue levels appear to be improving, but management fear that costs are going to ramp up to cope and thus expectations for profit growth will still be difficult to achieve.

What can banks do to manage costs better?

One approach is to follow the lead provided by manufacturing. Manufacturing has been facing relentless cost pressure for decades. They have faced outsourcing, offshoring, product obsolescence, currency moves etc. but many businesses remain profitable, even in the UK. Manufacturing has not maintained profitability by sporadic, half-hearted cost reduction projects or periodic bouts of headcount slashing. They have developed a mindset, methods and tools to identify and eliminate waste in all its forms at every opportunity and they have used approaches that involve their people and that bring them along with the changes. It is not about cost reduction; penny-pinching, cutting investment, taking out people; it is about finding better ways to get work done. It is about freeing-up resources because you no longer need to use them.

Resources that can be used to increase capacity to support business growth or to enable costs to be cut if that is what has to be done.

The mindset, methods and tools that manufacturing have developed to eliminate waste and thereby free-up resources are primarily:
1. Obtaining a clear understanding of what adds value to the customer.
2. Focusing on process flow and what causes time delays.
3. Analysing activities to identify the extent to which each contributes to customer value and then eliminating those activities that do not add value, i.e. eliminating waste.
4. Identifying and eliminating the root-cause of errors that impact the value adding activities.
5. Emphasising standardisation to achieve reliability in delivering quality.
6. Quantifying and eliminating the cost of complexity.

In our experience this manufacturing approach is effective in banking sector's processes in both the front and back office because mostly they are characterised by:
1. **Being slow:** The value add to lead-time ratio (that is the time spent adding value for a customer relative to the time from start to finish) is often less than 10%.
2. **Having many non-value-adding steps:** Most of the steps in financial service processes do not add value (in some cases in excess of 80%).

3. **Being over-engineered:** Many of the risk and compliance activities are in excess of what is required.
4. **Having excessive work in progress:** Many transactions spend most of their time in queues waiting processing, approval, further information etc.
5. **Having too many hand-offs:** Hand-offs from one person or department to another introduce time delays and error.

The manufacturing approach can be successfully tailored to engage the different types of people that work in financial services. Financial Services companies have a head start on Manufacturing because their managers and staff are, as a broad generalisation, more people orientated, more individualistic and have more freedom in the workplace to act and make decisions.

Chapter 9: The Principle of Lean Banking

As the CFO of a middle-market bank, you face mounting pressures inherent within your industry; both regulatory and economic. Daily, you battle against compressed margins due to lower interest rates (especially in commercial lending) and a shaky economy.

At least 40% of costs for financial services are a result of wasteful activities that provide no added value to your customer. In today's marketplace, it's much too risky to rely on your "gut" for decision-making. Lean banking data analysis is an evidence-based solution that provides you with a new view of your challenges to improve efficiency and data quality, effectively eliminating waste in your organization.

Lean processes are being adopted globally by organizations suffering from some level of inefficiency that is negatively affecting their bottom line. Post-recession, as the financial industry continues to resolve its credit and capital problems, many banks are now shifting their focus to improving operational efficiency.

The objective of a lean banking approach is to identify areas of waste and inefficiency within your organization and then apply proven methodologies to generate solutions. Lean middle-market banks enjoy improved customer experiences, get the most out of their staff, improve operational controls and reduce monetary waste wherever possible.

Lean banking is a low-cost way to eliminate non-value-added activities throughout all areas of your banking organization. As lean banking operations take shape, you set the stage to develop a company culture with the mindset for continuous streamlining of processes and improvements to operational efficiency.

The Path to Lean Banking Process Improvement

Many middle-market banks assume efficiency improvement should focus solely on overhead reduction. That is a start; however, to drive substantial lean banking process improvements, you need to improve revenue.

Over the last 10 years, drops in revenue rather than increases in overhead have driven declines in middle-market bank efficiency ratios. Therefore, your lean banking process improvement initiatives must include an analysis of sales and marketing, margin management, non-interest income management, as well as an ongoing review and improvement of these elements of lean banking operations.

The Benefits of Implementing Lean Banking Operations

Overlapping and/or inconsistent data, manual reporting, disparate systems and aging technology lead to poor information quality. Internally, your bank requires fast, accurate and increasingly transparent information to support smart, informed business decisions.

While lean banking helps you gain internal operational efficiency through fast and accurate banking data analysis, this process also satisfies the external needs of your organization (i.e. stakeholders and regulators who demand transparent, reliable information in less time).

Streamlined processes and operational efficiency lead to reduced costs and released capacity, meaning lean banking process improvement contributes significantly to your bottom line.

In fact, financial institutions leveraging lean banking operations report results of 20-30% cost reduction within 12 to 18 months and maintain cost-efficiency ratios below the industry average.

Lastly, unlike other banking process improvement methodologies, lean banking does not require significant capital investment. Lean middle-market banking concepts and tools are relatively easy to learn and apply.

Lean Banking Relies on Building A Client-Centred Organization

Banks have long-struggled to deliver excellent customer experience due to processes that are not geared toward the customers needs; this has hurt customer satisfaction overall.

Lean banking initiatives are rising rapidly in the financial sector, yet most banks' approaches are still too focused on cutting expenses. Real, lasting change requires your bank to focus on the cultural aspects of lean banking process improvement.

Think of lean banking as a behavioural change. Reduction of costs is just one benefit. To achieve a high-performing organization, combine lean banking operations with best practices that inspire your staff to deliver continuously excellent customer service.

Lean banking is all about improving process efficiency, performance management, organizational capabilities and the mindset and behaviours of your staff however, as you identify and remove non-value-added activities, your end-goal should always be focused on who the customers are and what they value, as they are a direct extension of your value stream.

Chapter 10: Using Cause and Effect Diagram

When organizations want to address an issue, they frequently bring people together to determine what actions to take. Often, part of the group's process is to brainstorm about what causes the issue to happen in the first place. Maybe you have been in one, or several, of these situations with your firm.

When faced with meetings around determining what causes a problem, we frequently find that many Lean Six Sigma process improvement teams don't get past the "Usual Suspects" to look for other root or contributing causes. Have you been in a situation like this where one of the early possibilities offered was around people, and the entire idea generation became identifying the guilty party? Or one where Training was identified as the cause and the group failed to look anywhere else?

A great Lean Six Sigma process tool to use for situations like this, to ensure you are really uncovering all the possible causes of issues, is the Cause and Effect Diagram. This tool is also referred to as a Fishbone Diagram, or Ishakawa diagram.

Using a Cause and Effect Diagram at a Financial Services Company

Lets use a simple example from the Financial Services field. This company assigns tasks to ensure that all customer queries are addressed appropriately. They have a set standard to address greater than 95% of those inquiries within 5 days. Many of these tasks require handing off to another person to address for further research. When people talked about tasks as a problem, a few of the frequent explanations were that "other areas don't care" and "people are lazy". Do either of those sound like familiar reasons used to describe any issues in your business?

Difficulty Meeting Their Standard.

The issue the financial company faced was that rather than 5% exceeding their standard, more than four times that much, 22% exceeded the five days. There was pressure put on the staff to work harder and make it happen, but the results did not move much.

Frustrated with the lack of movement, the group decided to gather a small team to determine what the causes behind the delays could be. This team had representatives of the areas responsible for both creating and completing the tasks. There were a couple of members of the supervisory team, but most team members were people that actually did the work.

The Cause and Effect Diagram to the Rescue

Rather than simply brainstorming a list of reasons, the team used a Cause and Effect (fishbone) diagram to ensure that they got out all the potential causes of the effect they were dealing with, the "late tasks". In a Cause and Effect, the effect you are attempting to understand is placed in a box that the right hand side of the diagram. It is important to agree of the effect you are trying to eliminate. Include information about the "what", "when", "how much" and "where" in your statement.

The tool is frequently called a fishbone, because categories are used to ensure the team fully explores the issues. These categories become the major bones of the fish. For this project, the team used the following six major bones for their fish:
1. Measures.
2. People.
3. Process.
4. Materials.
5. Equipment.
6. Environment.

As the group began to uncover potential causes, it became clear that there was a lot more going on than people not caring. As the group continued filing in the Cause and Effect, an active discussion took place around some of the systemic limitations that the representatives had to deal with in the tasking system. The group found contributing causes against every major bone of the fish. As with many other groups, they found there were multiple issues that contributed to the overall defect rate for the group.

One of the issues involved a certain type of tasks that by policy were put on a three-week delay before being completed. This accounted for over 5% of the tasks in excess of five days. The target of 95% completed within five days was not possible without changing this single policy even if all issues were completely removed. Calculating the responsiveness around tasks needed to take into account how long it took to complete the task when done properly.

By-products of Success

Another limiting factor was the lack of reporting and visibility around tasks in the system. Tasks were not separated in reporting by the type of task, to allow feedback around responsiveness. This issue was able to be resolved and with the increased awareness of the issues, some of the simpler tasks began to be followed up on more quickly. This change also led to creating clearer expectations and service level agreements between the departments around responsiveness for specific types of issues.

Multiple systems were a contributing factor and it was determined after further analysis that the majority of the issues came from one of the two systems. Using the Cause and Effect tool moved the discussion from the "usual suspects" to a fuller discussion and appreciation around the multiple causes contributing to the responsiveness to completing tasks.

Delivering Measurable Results; a 19% Improvement

We can report that the percent of tasks that can be completed within five days that are actually completed in that timeframe, improved to 97% at most recent count; a 19% improvement over the original completion rate and 2% higher than the standard goal.

Chapter 11: Leveraging Lean in Banking Sector

Not since the Great Depression has the financial services industry seen such disruption and upheaval as it has in recent years. Caught in such dire straits, firms often turn to drastic cost reduction measures to shore up the bottom line.

Unfortunately, doing so often means major reductions in workforce or a delayed start of strategic initiatives that could lead to new sources of revenue.

In 2009, companies in the S&P 500 displaced over 630,000 employees; 19%, or 121,000, were in the financial services industry.

In the past, large financial institutions were able to increase revenues through increased market share fuelled by mergers and acquisitions, and through total market growth.

In today's economy, however, firms no longer have the luxury of improving profit simply by increasing revenue. In addition, due to the significant headcount reductions in the financial services industry, these firms will need to improve operational efficiencies to merely support existing processes with fewer resources.

As a key indicator of operational cost in comparison to the revenue it generates, efficiency ratios at large financial institutions are flat at best. Efficiency ratio is generally calculated by dividing non-interest expense by total revenue less interest income. The target or ideal ratio is < 50% (lower is better).

In order to continue to meet shareholder expectations, financial services firms must take a focused look inward to eliminate waste and reduce operational costs.

A proven, effective way of doing this is to employ the same Lean techniques used by manufacturing firms for years. A 2007 study conducted by Technology Forecasters Inc. documented that 63% of the manufacturing companies surveyed reported lower overall costs as a benefit of Lean. In addition, 75% of the companies with advanced Lean programs enjoyed net profit margins greater than 5% of revenue, as compared to only 28% of non-adopters of Lean. Net profit margins at most global financial companies hover between 5% and 10%. With a fully developed Lean culture, it follows that these companies could see 10 - 15% margins.

So why have so few financial services firms tapped into the power of Lean to achieve this advantage?

Possible reasons include misconceptions about Lean's applicability outside of the manufacturing environment, or a perception that Lean may be a "bridge too far" for an organization gutted by layoffs. Regardless of their reasons for hesitating, financial services firms should no longer wait to embrace Lean transformation.

Identify the Opportunities

Organizational leaders in financial institutions may be wondering. How do I identify opportunities where an effective application of Lean could yield significant results? Fundamentally, Lean is about eliminating waste. Some waste is unavoidable, but the objective is to identify all activities that are non-value-added, and reduce as many as possible. General examples of waste include over-producing, waiting, defects/rework, over-processing, inventory, motion, and transport. A few specific examples of waste sometimes found in financial services include:
1. Rework due to lost files or processing errors.
2. Over-processing due to duplicate client records, or redundant data entry requirements.
3. Movement due to physical dispersion of process participants.
4. Printing, copying, and transporting of documents instead of transmitting/storing electronically.

Identifying, eliminating, or reducing such waste will enable firms to improve productivity, redeploy resources, increase customer satisfaction, and reduce costs. But waste can be pervasive and not easily identified. One Lean technique that can help uncover waste is Value Stream Mapping. A Value Stream Map (VSM) provides an end-to-end view of a process, as well as the availability, capacity, and performance of each step in the process. The VSM should include both physical flows and information flows. A Current State VSM shows the process as it is today and highlights opportunities to reduce waste in the current process. Future State VSMs depict how the process may look in the future, after improvements are implemented. This makes Value Stream Mapping a powerful visioning and communication tool.

An online survey of 920 executives of U.S. manufacturing and wholesale distributors, determined that 61% of companies surveyed are implementing Lean operating principles.

Value stream mapping can help uncover the process bottleneck. The bottleneck is the process step with the longest cycle time and is the step that determines the total output of the process. For example, common bottlenecks in a mortgage application approval process are the home inspection and/or appraisal. To increase output, either the cycle time of the bottleneck must be reduced or the available working time of the bottleneck must be increased.

In addition, bottlenecks should be protected from defects to maximize the usable output of that process. This may be achieved by implementing a test point, quality gate, or error proofing, just ahead of the bottleneck, to ensure that defective material does not exacerbate the bottleneck. By identifying, improving, and protecting bottleneck processes, financial services firms can improve their total operational efficiency and essentially "do more" with fewer resources.

Even after improving bottlenecks, we must understand the takt time to determine whether the process can meet customer demand. Takt time represents an increment of time used to demonstrate the frequency of customer demand. It is the cadence of customer demand.

To some, calculating takt time for processes inside a financial services company may seem unrealistic; however, many key functions such as bank teller services or delivery of investment advice by a call centre are both measurable and somewhat predictable. By determining takt time total demand for a product or service divided by the working time available to produce that product or service and tuning processes using Lean techniques to eliminate waste, work is performed more efficiently to a consistent pace of the takt.

Due to the nature of customer demand for financial services, a value stream will have various takt times depending on the month, day of the week or hour of the day. Companies that learn to leverage the concept of takt time to build capable processes that scale efficiently with the ebb and flow of demand will dramatically increase customer service levels and lower operational cost.

Chapter 12: Using Lean in Wholesale Banking

After achieving success using the lean-management approach in retail financial services, leading institutions are starting to utilize lean-management principles in their wholesale businesses. Some early adopters we know, recognizing that areas such as securities services and the processing of trades are ripe for change and have already achieved major improvements in accuracy, timeliness, efficiency, and even risk control; for instance, a reduction in the number of open items, and errors.

Yet some in the industry remain sceptical. First, the wholesale sector's profitability has historically depended on a constant stream of innovative expert-based, highly tailored, and high-margin products, so leaders may question whether lean's production-based insights apply to wholesale banking. Moreover, although the processes supporting those products usually start off as intensely manual, the industry has been at the forefront in the use of automation, outsourcing, and offshoring to reduce marginal costs as products mature. An understandable concern is that lean's process changes would upend vendor relationships or require yet another round of technology investments. Finally, some institutions we have seen are pursuing other efficiency initiatives that appear to incorporate similar ideas and fear that lean might interrupt them.

For a few banks, however, it is exactly this high-risk, highly complex environment that makes lean's comprehensive approach to minimizing waste and variability so valuable. By focusing on end-to-end processes rather than on individual activities or functions, lean allows institutions to see that they have many more "factory-like" work-streams than they may have realized. They then can adapt lean's traditional approach to each specific operation especially improving the alignment of operating teams, the balancing of capacity and workloads, and the transparency of information flows.

These changes allow institutions to use the investments they have already made in IT, outsourcing, or offshoring far more effectively. The impact can be dramatic. At one large asset manager we studied, for example, new fund-accounting processes reduced costs by 30 percent as error rates dropped by 75 percent. In the confirmation of derivatives, a global investment bank increased its efficiency by 40 percent while reducing errors by 50 percent and exposure to risky clients by 12 percent.

Lean makes processes more accurate, timely, and efficient with lower risk.

In the past several years, many wholesale banks we have observed have discovered the limits of relying exclusively on IT, outsourcing, and offshoring to reduce costs and increase efficiency. In IT, for example, the enormous technical challenges inherent in automation left little scope for project teams to revamp processes to take advantage of the new capabilities. Likewise, outsourcing and offshoring initiatives tended to concentrate on a narrow definition of value, as institutions swapped roles and activities in London or New York for similar ones in Zagreb or Hyderabad. Reallocating staff on a job-by-job or activity-by-activity basis meant that the only significant effect on costs was to lower employee salaries. Many institutions attempted to shift broken rather than well-functioning end-to-end processes to multiple offshore locations, where they were even more difficult to manage. As a result, at most wholesale banks we have studied, offshoring has reduced productivity rather than offered a competitive advantage.

Offshoring alone no longer seems to create a competitive advantage.

In many cases we have observed, even the savings from cheaper labour were offset by new, often-hidden costs of complexity; as files move from onshore employees to offshore employees to outsourced employees and back again, every step increases the risk of error and delay. Institutions are under greater scrutiny than ever from both clients and regulators, so accuracy has become even more critical. Yet in trying to mitigate these new quality concerns, institutions impose additional controls that reduce speed or add personnel further undercutting the returns from IT, outsourcing, and offshoring.

Resolving these conflicting pressures, we find, requires a breakthrough in managing wholesale-banking operations. Leading financial institutions are discovering that such a breakthrough is possible through the judicious application of lean principles; but that means assessing wholesale businesses from a new perspective, and the results are often a surprise. Viewed from end to end, the processes that underlie many of the most sophisticated wholesale products share essential features with factory workflows; low variability in tasks, narrow expertise requirements, predictable work, and limited interaction with third parties.

While few wholesale workflows involve all four features, many involve three enough for lean to have a real impact. In one bank's capital-market operations, for example, we found that about 25 to 30 percent of the workforce undertook routine "exception-based" activities, such as cash settlements; these employees intervened only when problems arose. Although this work is inherently unpredictable, it is almost exclusively internal, and the same exceptions occur repeatedly, limiting the variability of tasks and the range of expertise involved. Applying lean to these processes typically increased productivity by 20 to 25 percent. Likewise, an additional 35 to 40 percent of employees focused on "rules-based" work such as drafting documents. Tasks follow a fairly rigid set of requirements, with all the characteristics of lean except the final one, since these personnel must work closely with third parties. In this case, lean's productivity-improvement potential ranged from 15 to 25 percent.

Thus, 60 to 70 percent of the capital-market staff worked on processes in which lean could achieve substantial savings. Only a minority of employees had the highly customized client relationships or expert roles that are difficult to standardize.

Get it done

Once a wholesale institution commits itself to lean, a successful revamp rests on three of its core principles. The first is realigning teams to reflect value streams, or the steps involved in fulfilling a customer request, from initial receipt through completion. To minimize errors and to speed work from one specialist to the next, regardless of where each is located, the new configuration also eliminates functional boundaries. Thanks to that restructuring, an institution can use resources more effectively by rebalancing workloads. Finally, managers and employees must make information and metrics fully transparent to adjust the system appropriately to changing conditions.

Realign teams

The inherent complexity of wholesale processes raises challenges. At a given moment, managers may have only a limited view of basic operating conditions, such as the incoming workflow, the capacity of any work group, or total productivity. Backlogs form quickly, with significant rework arising from errors at earlier process stages. Units lack the flexibility to respond to new requests for example, to treat top clients differently or to process new products quickly. The fact that workers do not see each other may exacerbate the problems by weakening the sense of mutual accountability.

Nevertheless, geographic dispersion is a critical element of the solution. A typical lean move is to organize employees into teams, or "work cells," whose organization more closely matches the process steps they undertake and fosters stronger relationships and responsibility among team members. Under this structure, one group of employees from related job functions, who typically would have separate reporting lines, is responsible for every step involved in fulfilling a customer request. While the employees in such a cell often work in the same location, wholesale banks can take advantage of their current outsourcing and offshoring models to create "virtual" work cells that maximize talent cost advantages. In short, outsourcing and offshoring let institutions find the right talent at the right price, while lean allows them to use talent in the most effective way.

In our experience, lean can also help institutions identify targeted opportunities to use outsourcing and offshoring more effectively. An international bank, for example, cut across organizational and physical boundaries in a unit responsible for processing dividends, stock splits, and the like. It created new cross-functional teams that reduced the average age of the unit's breaks by almost 20 percent and the related risk by more than 50 percent.

What is more, by applying lean's end-to-end perspective in revamping the underlying processes, the bank found that one of its offshore facilities had become so experienced in several necessary tasks that it could become a "centre of excellence." The bank therefore shifted about 30 percent of the unit's full-time-equivalent positions to that facility. As a result, several of the original unit's oversight functions became redundant. The number of full-time-equivalent employees in it fell by 14 percent.

Rebalance workloads

Once the new teams are in place, managers can start balancing workloads much more productively and thereby address chronic mismatches between the supply of and demand for labour throughout wholesale financial processes. A global investment bank we studied was typical; breaks in derivatives settlement were accumulating faster than it could resolve them, allowing needless risk exposures and undermining client service guarantees. At a large US asset manager, fund accountants found themselves in a daily fire fight, rushing to integrate data before reporting deadlines, although low-value tasks consumed the rest of their work hours.

The techniques involved in readjusting workflows mostly apply familiar lean themes, starting with a detailed analysis of employee activities and of production demands. Once managers eliminate obvious waste, they can assess the capacity and capabilities of an operations staff, identifying opportunities to shift less urgent tasks to less busy time slots or to create separate channels for activities involving larger risks or requiring greater judgment. Such changes increased the productivity of the global investment bank's back office for settlements by 15 to 25 percent (depending on product type) and helped it reduce its error rate by 15 percent. The asset manager freed up more than two-and-a-half hours of each fund accountant's day, enabling these employees to meet their deadlines more consistently and speeding up their work by over 40 percent.

Make data transparent

The final requirement is to review the way work status updates proceed through the organization. In complex operations, an employee whose work relies on earlier stages in a process often has no way of knowing if the team responsible for completing them has run into obstacles and been delayed. A critical component is therefore to improve communication between up and downstream information flows, regardless of location. The asset manager realized this goal by using a new system of video screens that help each employee track the status of a particular task at a particular time. Such visual techniques allow managers and employees to respond quickly to problems as they arise. If, for example, a data feed goes down, all team members relying on it know in real time and can cooperate on finding alternatives that enable everyone to meet their deadlines.

An integrated solution

One institution's derivatives confirmation operation illustrates how the three components come together. Before a lean transformation, the execution of a "plain vanilla" equity derivative required an average of 37 days as it slowly progressed from one functional group to the next, crossing several time zones along the way. The institution started by reorganizing its processing front line into virtual work cells that assumed responsibility for particular groups of clients. It also simultaneously implemented new workload-balancing tools that enabled it to shift tasks among the work cells as demand volume changed, thus preventing the backlogs that had been a crucial source of error. The third component was a continuously updated, fully transparent performance-data system that enforced accountability by allowing each employee to see where the cell stood at any time compared with its targets. These changes together allowed the institution to reduce delays by 40 percent and to increase client satisfaction significantly.

Build buy-in

Because of the sensitivity of the processes involved, managing such changes will be especially demanding.

Two factors are critical.

The first need is a deep commitment from the leadership. Although we find that designing and implementing a lean program is often far less expensive than alternatives based on IT or on outsourcing and offshoring, internal resistance to lean can be even greater because employees may fear that by "industrializing" operations, it will diminish the value of their contributions. Leaders must therefore emphasize that waste prevents employees from fully using their skills.

Thorough prototyping is the second requirement. To be comfortable making risky changes in processes, we find that organizations must experience a prototype operating in a live, working environment, with ordinary employees doing actual work on actual products. By demonstrating what lean can achieve, this sort of pilot generates excitement at all levels of an organization as people recognize how lean can improve their jobs. At the asset manager, for example, before the lean transformation most accountants handled about 11 funds each. Employees who worked with the prototype eventually reached 16 funds, while errors dropped by 75 percent and total reporting cycle time declined by 25 percent.

The first step in achieving these sorts of improvements is for leaders to look hard at wholesale operations, particularly those where cost pressures may be rising as returns from IT and outsourcing and offshoring projects diminish. Reimagining these work-streams can bring new value from long-standing investments and create new opportunities.

Chapter 13: Cutting Costs While Reducing Risks

The financial services sector has been a laggard in adopting lean tools and practices, perhaps because of their manufacturing origins. But those attitudes are slowly changing. As more banks discover the benefits of lean operations; such as lower costs, fewer errors, faster cycle times and far greater efficiency wide-scale adoption by the industry is just a matter of time. But old habits often die hard, and slowly.

Opportunity and Challenges

For process-oriented industries such as financial services, lean holds enormous potential. Lower costs and fewer errors are just the beginning. Banks that take on successful lean programs often see a 15% to 25% improvement in efficiency. Gains in cycle time can be even more dramatic, with improvements of 30% to 60% possible. Lean thinking can even help management understand which customer groups are most profitable and where service can be enhanced most cost-effectively. The results of lean initiatives can be dramatic.

An international commercial bank discovered the potential for 30% more efficiency in processing customer transactions while improving customer satisfaction through more differentiated service.

A lean audit of one North American asset manager uncovered ways to make product pricing 12% - 20% more efficient by carefully identifying and eliminating non-value added activities.

Analysts using a lean approach in one investment bank reportedly gained 20% - 30% in analyst productivity and a 60% reduction in cycle time by redefining credit processes.

Given this potential, why hasn't lean made more inroads in the financial services industry? We argues that human nature blocks progress.

Most service companies tend to be in denial that lean applies to their industry. Typically, everyone agrees it's great for manufacturing, and then denies it could work in their business. A few years later perhaps after a competitor has shown some success with a lean approach some managers concede that lean could work, but only in the back office and other lower-value parts of the operation. Finally, years later, the whole workforce will reorganize. I can't help but see a pattern here.

In fact, lean for manufacturing and lean for finance are not all that different, Finance is just a different kind of factory. It is a processing factory, and there is a lot of waste. The basic philosophy doesn't really change.

Becoming lean involves eliminating the "seven deadly sins" of waste in a process; overproduction, waiting, poor transportation/logistics, over-processing, suboptimal inventory control, rework, and unneeded movement. People exposed to lean thinking are trained to see and remove these wasteful practices. As superfluous steps are managed away, the process becomes more efficient. Waste begins to disappear. Speed improves and costs drop.

Another key principle of lean is to focus on what is important, what matters to the customer, what delivers value. Almost everything else should be cut; but understanding what customers value isn't always easy, especially when functional silos isolate employees from the front line or the marketplace. Very often, employees get ideas about what is important to the customer based on limited knowledge or an incomplete understanding of customer needs.

Often, lean thinking helps give executives a broader perspective on a process, making it easier to see possibilities for improvements than a more silo-bound view traditionally did.

Changing Mindsets and Attitudes

Lean thinking is nothing new, of course, but more banks have talked about it than tried it. Far more common is an attempt to cut costs without undertaking an actual lean program. "Lean isn't simply about cost cutting, but about changing the way you work.

While the basic idea of lean is familiar to many financial executives, getting them to follow through is another matter. It's like your diet. You know what to eat, I know what to eat, it's not that hard to know, but you don't eat it. You come home, you are tired from work, and you have a beer! I think the same is true for lean. Old habits are hard to break.

Many banks that have applied lean to back-office processing have reached a steady state followed by diminishing returns. But there is a second stage of opportunity in higher-level processes, such as those that touch the customer in branches or the front-office. Still, many executives in those areas continue to deny that lean can improve their productivity. They will say, "Well, lean doesn't apply to me. It's just the $45,000 a year underwriter, the simple banker in the branch office who should do lean. I am special."

Part of the reluctance may have to do with lean's shop-floor origins. Some executives may equate lean to dumbing down a job. Others mistakenly think lean requires standardizing every part of a process; but it doesn't. "It's more about getting smarter about what you do."

In fact, getting lean often requires creative thinking. For example, when paperwork moves online, the steps of a financial process are often still performed in a sequential order, even when they could be done in parallel. So forget the assembly line approach. Think more like a race-car pit crew, and process speed can improve dramatically.

This kind of creative thinking often exposes a great deal of waste. At one major consumer bank we work with only 40% of the labour that went into loan underwriting added any value. The rest was frittered away on such unproductive activities as processing loans that were unlikely to be accepted by customers because the bank had taken too long to respond, or processing loans that should have been rejected because the applicant's credit status was obviously too low, and trying repeatedly but unsuccessfully to reach customers on the telephone.

Managing Risks

Like any major improvement effort, lean is not risk-free. As systems grow more efficient, warns, quality control and risk management must improve along with them.

In a system with no slack, a single defect in one item can easily snowball into a much larger problem. Just as manufacturers that work on a lean, zero-inventory basis must have assurances from suppliers that their parts will have zero defects, banks with lean operations must put in place strict quality controls. In particular, automatic systems must be watched closely to ensure that they don't exacerbate a difficult market by, say, withdrawing credit at the wrong time.

We believes that lean most often reduces risk. Lean is one of the very effective ways to actually mitigate operational risk, much of which arises from errors at the front line. By standardizing processes and empowering front-line people, managers can cut out a lot of that risk.

Standardization can also reduce errors. For example, in cash reconciliations; You are basically taking two entries, trying to compare them, and lowering the bank's exposure if there is a mismatch. In the average big bank, many small groups perform separate reconciliations, using different technologies, processes and standards. That can lead to mistakes.

This lack of coordination can be costly, particularly when allowed to continue long-term. With lean, you can standardize, you can homogenize, you can roll up uniform processes and significantly cut exposure.

Getting It Right

The best way to begin a lean program is to map an entire end-to-end process, then look for ways to streamline it. You are much more likely to be successful carving up and defining specific processes with a beginning point and an endpoint.

You need to focus first on some pragmatic, easily implemented and meaningful applications of change. Once these are shown to be a success, you can build momentum. It's a marathon.

Analysis and implementation are extremely different. In theory, lean tools and techniques are pretty simple but the execution; getting to success is complex. One reason; it is a people process, and it requires a big change in the culture and in the way you manage activities.

Although implementing lean begins as an operations issue, it quickly becomes a change management exercise that requires companies to deal with workers in new, unfamiliar ways. For instance, the lean principle of engaging employees in problem-solving means that workers involved in a process must be asked how it might be simplified or improved. You can't just say, Let's run this exercise and we will worry about the people dimension later. Managing change and people's behaviours is a continuous process that must be addressed from day one. Managers may see this as slowing down the lean effort, but ultimately it can simplify their task and improve the eventual outcome. Employees are more likely to resist new approaches if they don't understand how they can help improve the process overall or how their effort adds value.

While it might be tempting to simply issue an edict and try to order a lean program; what works best is to engage workers early on. Lean works best as a balanced top-down and bottom-up effort. The organization needs to share a common goal and set of expectations of value that the lean program will deliver, and have the executive commitment and appropriate governance to enable its success; however, you also want to heavily involve front-line workers and encourage them to share their ideas. You want to let them know that it's okay for them to speak up, and that they should drive the definition, testing and validation of the new process.

Done right, lean isn't a one-off project but instead a pervasive approach to operations that brings lasting cultural change. It transforms the way employees view their work by encouraging them to continually think about ways to improve it. They are not just there to punch the clock and do what they are told. Do not overlook this need for change management. It is incredibly important to do. Otherwise, lean just becomes a project and a one-time event, and the costs and the risks will creep back in a few years.

Limits of Lean

Lean does have its limits. One of its core principles and a key part of process optimization is to minimize variability, which reduces errors and improves quality; but going lean would not be a good way to run a fire department. You might say it's totally inefficient that these guys are getting paid to sit in the station 80% of the time. Wouldn't it be better to make sure that they are always busy and that the fire truck is fully utilized? But it just doesn't work that way, because unless you are the one causing the fires, a fire department needs to hold excess capacity!

An extremely lean system is very vulnerable to external shocks to the system; strikes or traffic jams, bad weather, earthquakes, whatever messes up the system.

The challenge of using lean in a service business is that the customer is much more closely connected to what is being produced. In effect, the customer is often the object moving through a service process, and that complicates matters immensely.

Imagine you are running a travel office. The perfect lean team might get its processes right and do everything consistently, but suppose a customer wants to talk for 30 minutes before booking a flight? The process may not allow for such lengthy conversations. That is why, intrinsically, the application of lean is harder in services.

What is Next

For many banks, the first item on the lean agenda may be to increase the value and productivity of a merger or an acquisition. People are revisiting those partially integrated units, looking for next-generation synergies in operating models and work processes.

Lean thinking may also be moving up the value chain in finance, as it has in other service industries. As an example, lean thinking could be applied to investment operations to streamline processes and speed up decision-making. I see absolutely no reason why lean tools shouldn't be applied to more knowledge-intensive processes.

Chapter 14: Application of Lean to Financial Services

Lean isn't about manufacturing. It is about standardizing work processes to make problems visible and developing your team members' critical thinking ability so that they can solve those problems and improve work processes.

If you are part of a service organization, how often have you heard someone say, "We can't do lean here. Lean is just for manufacturing, isn't it? We are not some kind of widget-making assembly line, putting one piece onto another every 10 seconds! Our processes are long and complex; every transaction is unique and requires special consideration and besides, most of the work we do takes place in our peoples' minds and behind their computer screens. There is no possible way we could use lean here."

Having spent many years helping different types of service organizations implement lean, you can imagine how many times I have heard a version of this statement and over the years, what I have come to realize is that it is precisely because service processes do tend to have long cycle times (think quarterly payroll tax processes), many complex variables, multiple decision points and interactions with a variety of computer systems (think putting someone on a short-term disability leave of absence) and much of the value-added work does often take place out of sight, in peoples' minds (think call centre reps answering complicated HR-related questions) that makes lean philosophy and tools a great fit and can be of huge benefit for services industries. Since service processes are not physically observable, especially useful are tools like visual management that make otherwise invisible work processes visible, and techniques that specifically develop a team member's creative problem-solving and critical thinking abilities to the fullest.

If your service organization currently doesn't practice lean, and you don't believe me, try this little experiment. Find a team that does similar work, such as entering customer transactions or answering customer calls. Give each team member a different coloured pad of post-it notes and choose one particular process all team members complete regularly. Ask each team member to write the series of steps that he or she takes to do the work on a separate post-it note. Once all have completed their post-its, have each team member stick their series of notes; one row for each team member, one above the other onto a large piece of paper or a whiteboard.

Oh, and by the way, make sure to ask the team beforehand if they think each of them is completing the sequence of steps the same way. I assure you that they will all say that they are positive they are doing the same set of steps, and that all the rows of post-it notes will be the same length and contain the same number of steps performed in the same order.

After completing the exercise, take a step back, and take a look. I can absolutely guarantee that none of the rows will be the same length, or have the same steps in the same order.

This is precisely why it is even more important for service organizations with long, complex, variable processes with multiple decision points to use the tools that lean gives us to make processes that take place inside people's heads visible. If all of your team members aren't doing the work in the same way, each and every time, how can you guarantee that your customers are getting consistent high-quality services each and every time? If your team members are not constantly pushing their critical thinking skills to improve the process, how can you guarantee that they will be able to respond to increasing levels of complex service requests interacting with multiple departments and complicated systems to make the right decisions to satisfy your customers and keep them from going to the competition?

Now you can use this same post-it note exercise to develop a visible standard process for doing the work shown by person. You can estimate times for tasks and establish a daily cadence for work. When there are deviations between what you expect to happen and what does happen, you have an opportunity for improving the process.

Lean isn't about manufacturing. It is about standardizing work processes to make problems visible and developing your team members' critical thinking ability so that they can solve those problems and improve work processes. So the next time someone in your service organization tries to tell you that "lean is just for manufacturing," you will know better.

Chapter 15: Implementing Lean in a Banking Sector

As a result of the 2008 economic crisis, most financial bodies made significant emergency cutbacks in order to keep afloat during turbulent times. Now, years later, those same organizations realize that they need a more comprehensive and strategic plan to cope with the business reality which has developed since that crisis.

This reality check has left companies facing harsh challenges, such as reduced profit margins, accelerated competition and greater consumer awareness. Decidedly out of their comfort zones, these companies are under pressure to develop and maintain comprehensive organizational processes, involving substantial changes to the way in which services are provided, a deeper understanding of how service value is perceived by customers and a closer focus on exactly how these services can be maximized to increase this value for both the customer and the company.

According to an updated survey conducted among managers of U.S. banks and financial organizations, 43% of the respondents thought that bank managers should devote the next two years to initiatives for improving operational efficiency, reducing costs and inspecting their operative and organizational model.

A cross-organizational analysis of this scale and significance requires a powerful method of application. One of the leading approaches employed is based on "lean" principles.

The lean method

Lean is a managerial approach which inspects processes, services and products according to their value from the customer's perspective.

The methodology is based on five basic principles

Proper implementation of the methodology enables the organization to achieve constant long-term improvement. Profits are maximized by concentrating on products and services which are valuable to the customer and costs are minimized by eliminating "waste" in the process and reducing operations which do not add value. With a clear focus on process standardization, quality improvement, cost cuts and efficiency enhancement, the lean method has recently been gaining momentum and crossing over from its traditional base in industry to various branches of service organizations. According to a recent survey, 17% of the organizations which have implemented this methodology over the past few years are service organizations.

The potential of this method for process-oriented organizations, such as financial institutes, is enormous. Not only can they profit from lower costs and error rates, successful implementation of the lean approach can bring a 15% - 25% improvement in efficiency and a 30% - 60% increase in Cycle time.

Most major banks around the world have already begun to implement lean principles and have:
1. Improving customer experience by strengthening the interface for the customer in all channels.
2. Improving services and products and adapting them to customer needs.
3. Reducing costs (fixed and variable).
4. Shortening cycle time and improving their efficiency.
5. Measuring performance at real time.

The implementation of this approach in banks is also expressed by performing customer segmentation and mapping the value offered in each segment. This has had an impact on branch formats, with opening hours being adjusted to customer needs and operating centres being established, to reduce the workforce in branches and focus on core operations.

Where do we begin? (setting into motion)

The decision to implement the lean approach at your bank is a significant strategic step. This will need to be backed up with all the required resources and support to ensure its successful completion. You should also be aware that it will take courage to make what may be substantial changes for your organization, particularly in relation to its core sectors.

How do we begin? (work stages)

We begin this stage with customer segmentation. This involves.
1. Defining segment groups according to behavioural characteristics in the world of services. For example: technologically oriented as too personal relations / VIP etc.
2. Analysis of the bank's customer population according to the defined segments and analysis of the "typical" customer in each segment.
3. Analysis of customer needs for each segment, including product, means of approach, manner of providing service etc.
4. Formulating USP (unique selling proposition) while taking into account the bank's potential for profit.

We then need to define an operating model.

This should support the bank's core operations, namely sales and customer service, with a view to maintain the bank's profit goals and reaching a state of constant streamlining.

The optimum model for implementation of lean principles composed of the following elements.
1. Changing the branches to focus on consultation and sales.
2. Diverting customers to direct channels for performing simple actions and receiving services.

3. Establishing service and operating centres which perform back office, sales support operations and services instead of the branches.
4. Establishing excellence centres for giving a professional response to various subjects which require specialization.

The primary significance of this model is to remove certain operations from the branches to one of the supporting channels, so that branch employees have more time for focusing on value added activities.

This process of transferring operations is not only technical. It includes an opportunity to thoroughly inspect processes, make processes leaner and more efficient, cancelling and reducing steps that do not add value for the customer, standardizing the performance of the process and preventing repeat actions, reducing/cancelling controls, etc. In some cases, process inspection can lead to the entire process being removed.

Building the infrastructure

Building the infrastructure to support the process is complex and involves many channels.

1. Detailed characterization of the operating model:
    a. Define branch operations by process, sector, subject, and customers segment.
    b. Define joint centre structure and work methods.

    c. Define branch interfaces and work methods in conjunction with centres

2. Workforce changes:
    a. Plan and estimate number of employees required to perform operations in joint centres versus number of employees required in branches, where workload has been cut.
    b. Build plan for transfer of workforce from branches to centres, based on skills and bank's needs.
    c. Formulate plans for early employee retirement where necessary.

3. IT support:
    a. Find technological solutions and expertise for successful implementation of the approach and operating model. Update work plans and direct resources to where they are needed (recruiting more if necessary).

4. Detailed characterization of work processes:
    a. Inspect and analyze processes and topics transferred to centres and define optimal work process. This includes interfaces to the branches, data system requirements, process controls, indicators etc. Maintain lean principles to create efficient and streamlined processes in branches and centres

5. Instruction and training:
    a. Formulate means of instruction and training for all branches and centres; concentrated

training for employees, implementation teams in branches and centres, etc.
b. Define training content for branches and centres.

6. Construction and real estate:
a. Reduce the physical size of branches and locate areas for new joint centres.

The organizational effort required to build an infrastructure in line with the work plan, as well as allocating resources and synchronizing individual elements demands good overall management of the process. We recommend using the following organizational infrastructures to.

Leading, managing and control:
a. Establish a body responsible for management, lead and control of progress.
b. Establish a steering committee for key decisions, to include senior managers from all bodies, businesses and operating areas involved.
c. Define a detailed work plan for implementation, management routines, control and escalation of progress.
d. Establish work teams for each sector.

Integrating mixed units:
a. Allocate a body responsible for each mixed unit.
b. Define areas of responsibility, functions and level of contribution required of each party involved.

Implementation

1. Implementation while in motion

Implementation of the lean approach and the operating model covers a wide variety of operations and areas across units and branches. It takes time to build all the infrastructure required. Nevertheless, to reap rewards from the process, even at the early stages, specific work packages for short term realization should be defined. This maintains the basic implementation principle; "implementation while in motion". This means that the team need to work in parallel, continuing to implement long term work packages while characterizing and developing future work packages.

2. Deployment plan for branches and centres

Parallel to defining work packages for removal of processes from the branches, a deployment plan needs to be developed to ensure that these processes are delegated to the correct centres. In detail, this schedule defines the pace of terminating branch processes and moving employees to the centres. In addition to operating importance, this plan clarifies and presents the bank management's commitment to the wider process.

3. Change management and communication

The success of such a wide-ranging process will be measured by means of two main indicators; customer satisfaction and the quantity of resources saved. The first indicator is subjective. In reality, customer satisfaction is measured in those "moments of truth" when the customer needs bank services. Add to this the banker's satisfaction and the message the customer receives from that banker.

We cannot stress enough the importance of the communication channels and the management of change which accompanies this step, both in presenting the change and twice in giving the correct messages which reflect the lean approach to customers and bank employees alike.

Correct formulation of these messages, both internally and externally, contributes significantly to the success of the process. It is therefore important to clarify the factors influencing these channels and to review the situation with every central operation performed.

The implementation of such a wide-scale process undoubtedly constitutes an enormous challenge. For the process to succeed, the business, operating and human elements involved must work together perfectly.

The business component includes logical formation of the approach and the operating model. The operations to be removed from the branches must be clearly defined and their value in the eyes of the customers understood. Courage is required to break away from traditional paradigms, conceptions and clearly defined responsibilities are essential to ensure that the new "products" are developed correctly.

The operating component involves establishing the management team, implementing management routines, formulating a deployment plan, work plans, tracking and control.

The human component focuses on transparency, routine communication of successes, matching human resources to operations, establishing centres with quality spearheading forces and including employees in the process right from the early stages.

The correct combination of these components, with the assistance of external support to help discard old paradigms and breaking through new paths, will help your organization build the infrastructure for constant improvement and for attaining the required efficiency objectives.

Chapter 16: Incremental Implementation

How a bank introduces and follows through on lean is equally critical to the effort's success. Many banks take what amounts to a one-time, big-bang approach, often led by experts ("black belts" and "master black belts"), and assume that the problem will be solved. This typically generates gains, but the gains are short-lived. Once the black belts leave, the organization reverts to its old patterns and behaviours.

Far better results can be achieved, in our experience, through an incremental approach based on a series of pilots. Such a "do-learn-do" approach allows a bank to produce quick wins and "mini-transformations," one process at a time, to set the stage and build momentum for a broader transformation.

The series of mini-transformations should be rapid and should target processes where results can be achieved quickly that is, in under six months and where transformation will have the largest and broadest impact. The approach should also be designed to be minimally invasive, allowing implementation of the program without a disruption of the target processes' day-to-day operations.

Within each mini-transformation, the focus should be on optimizing value levers to eliminate waste, reduce variability, and ultimately maximize system-wide performance. Enablers such as information technology, which can allow the automation of many tasks resulting in fewer processing errors, shorter cycle times, and a freeing up of manpower to focus on higher-value-added activities should be incorporated into the effort, and lean tools such as kaizen and value-stream mapping should be utilized heavily to identify improvement opportunities and solutions.

The transformations can be structured to deliver benefits in three waves. The first wave is the delivery of quick wins (for example, process improvements and quick system fixes) and the establishment of momentum. The second wave involves breaking down broader organizational barriers (for example, risk policies and procedures), engaging more personnel, and gaining buy-in for the full rollout. The third wave encompasses more difficult actions (such as decisions about outsourcing or offshoring and more comprehensive IT changes) and the full rollout.

Chapter 17: Lean Approach to Big Data

The proliferation of so-called 'big data' and the increasing capability and reducing cost of technology are very seductive for retail financial services organisations seeking to improve their customer engagement and operational performance; but many simply do not appreciate the real costs in terms of money and time that burden 'big' approaches to big data programmes and very few understand that the strength and quality of customer engagement bear little relation to the tools that have been bought.

Rather than rushing into big data programmes, organisations need to invest in a 'lean' approach to data and analytics, which will align all business capabilities, including strategy, people, processes and technology, towards a more socially connected customer.

A lean approach will help organisations focus only on the data needed to deliver specific business outcomes. The insights they extract will allow customers to engage with their bank or insurer in innovative and exciting ways. For the organisation, lean can help improve productivity and efficiency. It can also help to create a lasting and memorable brand in our increasingly digital world. With a little of creative thinking and a focused, lean approach, organisations can create a positive groundswell of support in favour of their products and services. Lean offers something unique and inspiring, something that connects with customers and inspires loyalty and trust.

Beware the promise of big data

Data volume and complexity are exploding. Firms in the financial services sector, like almost all organisations, are coming under increasing pressure to exploit so-called 'big data' to enhance service differentiation, reduce risk and improve performance.

They are implementing large-scale data analytics programmes to make use of the burgeoning quantities of information available in the expanding 'digital universe'. Such programmes seek to collect, store, manage and analyse data from a range of sources to identify insights that can be used to help decision-making.

When you take a look at the digital universe, it is easy to see why organisations are so interested. A research company, released its fifth digital universe report last year in which it claimed that the total amount of data created and replicated in 2011 would exceed 1.8 zettabytes; an amount equivalent to a stack of books stretching from the Earth to Pluto and back ten times.

Much of this data is created by individuals, using social networks to connect with other people and organisations in new and exciting ways.

Everyday, for instance, we send 294 billion emails and

share one billion items on Facebook; every minute we post 170,000 'tweets' to Twitter, 3,000 photos to Flickr and 48 hours of video to YouTube.

In the mobile world, there are now more than five billion mobile phones. Consumer demand is also booming for other mobile devices, ranging from tablets and eBook readers to smartphones and wireless-enabled cameras.

By 2020, researchers forecasts that the digital universe will have grown nearly 20-fold to contain approximately 35 zettabytes of data.

For financial institutions, big data is now seen as a strategic imperative for dealing with the acute stress of renewed economic uncertainty, increasing regulation, proposed banking sector reforms and the legacy of customer mistrust following Payment Protection Insurance mis-selling and the credit crisis of 2008.

Big data does not automatically deliver big value

As data warehouses start to overflow, and as the need for more relevant and timely analysis begins to put strain on traditional business intelligence tools, firms cannot afford to get carried away with the marketing hype surrounding big data.

On the other hand, data is absolutely necessary to provide the evidence to support new customer engagement initiatives. Several firms in both banking and insurance have recently launched new initiatives that attempt to engage customers in new ways, particularly in the online or mobile worlds. While such initiatives may appear attractive in the short term, how can firms sustain these activities in an efficient and effective manner without using data to measure their success?

Big data programmes are not without risk, especially for organisations already struggling in today's complex and highly regulated operating environment. They can either become misdirected by their singular focus on data volume, variety and velocity, or the initiatives lack the necessary supporting evidence needed to make them successful.

Converting big data programmes into successful activities that deliver meaningful business insight and provide sustained high-quality customer relationships can be costly, risky and sometimes fruitless. Although managing the increasing complexity of data is critical to the future success of the organisation, new initiatives should concentrate only on what is necessary to achieve the required business outcomes.

Big data hype also tempts organisations to seek new external sources of data, with particular emphasis these days on social media; but according to recent big data research by the Economist Intelligence Unit, more than 75 per cent of senior executives from over 500 companies say that they are wasting more than half the data they already hold and if the Pareto principle holds; that is, 80 per cent of the value comes from 20 per cent of the data then in their haste to embrace new external data sources, firms are potentially missing out on significant value.

Organisations do find it hard to deal with their enterprise data because their IT estates are too difficult to navigate compared to the openness of the Internet, for example. Mergers and acquisitions, as well as legacy systems developed decades ago, have created 'brown-field' environments in which valuable data is often locked up in organisational 'stove-pipes'.

The net result is that big data activities can all too easily focus on data which has the lowest potential to add value, thus wasting time, cost and effort.

Firms are caught between a rock and a hard place

Buying in great swathes of new technology and importing new data will improve inputs rather than outputs, while services provided to customers will remain utilitarian and transactional in nature.

In addition, strategic impact will be hard to achieve through point-to-point interactions that fail to provide the firm with a complete and accurate view of the customer; but without an injection of big data, retail financial services will become increasingly boring and customers will lose interest and trust. Firms will lose revenue.

Big data has become a mantra for all organisations interested in improving their performance and gaining competitive advantage. So how should the retail financial services sector approach it?

Is big data even the right place to start looking for a new customer experience?

Rather than collecting more data, and spending more time and money managing it, firms must use their existing enterprise data in combination with other sources of highly targeted data in a more intelligent way. They must adopt a new 'lean' approach to big data, which is more appropriate to continuing uncertain economic conditions and the modern needs of the new 'connected customer'.

Organisations need to invest in a lean approach to data and analytics, which aligns all business capabilities, including strategy, people, processes and technology.

Firms are now presented with the opportunity to become accessible and direct like never before. Social networks and the new generation of smartphones enable customers to use and interact with firms whenever they want and from wherever they may be.

Data and analytics that enable firms to focus on connected customers have the potential to create the greatest strategic impact. By taking this approach, rather than having a blind focus on big data, financial institutions can withstand the increasing external pressures faced by their retail divisions and look forward to a future in which they listen, learn and engage better with their customers.

Chapter 18: Making Lean Work

Banks can learn from the automobile industry's success in applying Lean production practices to gain efficiency and improve quality.

Financial institutions operate many areas that resemble automobile manufacturing plants. The processing involved in loan origination or payments operations, for example, involves multiple steps, carried out by specialized staff, and chained together to create a meta-process that can span the whole enterprise. The end product has two values associated with it; the value to the customer, and the value (cost) that the institution placed on the work to create it. Unfortunately, in many cases, the latter cost is higher than the value placed on the product by the customer.

Gaining the Benefits of Lean

The similarity between automobiles and banking is good news for the financial services industry because it implies that Lean production practices can be applied to complex operations at the bank to gain efficiency and improve quality. Lean production has been proven to gain efficiencies and increase quality across multiple dimensions that can benefit banks, including.

1. Finding Waste: Wasted processing and manpower immediately come to light using a Lean analysis. Excess work, unnecessary re-work, and idle time due to "choke points" (where one department cannot proceed until the preceding group releases work to it) are identified and can be eliminated, many times with minor changes and drastic improvements.

2. Eliminating Variances: Variances between work arrival and staffing levels are revealed, leading to better workforce capacity planning. Managers can accurately staff for anticipated work periods without overstaffing in order to ensure that service levels can be met. In some cases, the actual work processes are found to have steps that contain large variances. These can be reengineered to smooth the work flow.

3. Quantifying Cost and Value: Cost-to-value is now quantifiable, allowing accurate analysis for returns on investments for new programs or process changes. Empirical data collection is used to model changes with a high level of confidence, before the changes are executed. This data can also be used to improve pricing for existing and new products in the market.

4. Improving Workforce Performance: Individual and departmental staff performance is improved. Using empirical and consistent data, staff and managers can have objective and transparent discussions about individual performance, leading to improved work quality and the creation of best practices using real life experiences. Lean practices also place an emphasis on a holistic view of production, so individual staff members feel more like a critical part of a bigger process.

The resulting improvements lower the cost to "produce" the end product while increasing the value to the customer, through faster production and increased quality.

A Lean Case Study

One $60 billion, U.S. based full-service bank learned how well Lean is applicable in financial services. With more than 9,000 employees including 1,500 staff in the back office; the bank created models in order to estimate the workforce's efficiency. The models revealed significant waste in the bank's back office. An analysis of one area in the back office showed a 10 percent difference between payroll and actual productive work by that department staff was being paid 40 hours for only 36 hours of work. Worse, there were some areas in the bank's back office that had no data on where the workforce was actually spending its time.

The bank created a disciplined workforce management strategy, using Lean at its core, to improve the value it was providing to the customer through cost reductions and improved customer service. Former auto engineers were brought in to leverage their experience in Lean production strategies within the bank's operations areas. The team, made up of engineers and bank executives, started with Activity-Based Costing (ABC) to quantify the inefficiencies reported by the earlier models. ABC determines exactly what every widget costs to make or in the bank's case, what every activity in a process costs in terms of full-time employee (FTE) hours or payroll dollars.

In order to gather the data critical to ABC, the bank implemented a comprehensive workforce management solution consisting of software and new processes. This included touch-screen kiosks where staff checked in and out every day to collect workforce performance and process data. Prior to the introduction of the kiosk, workers clocked in and out but there was no centralized accounting for what the staff did during their day. By tying this to production systems, the result was an exact measurement of workforce productivity and the efficiency of the processes overall. Combined with payroll system data, it provided insight into costing, individual and departmental productivity and performance, capacity, and more.

ABC was the key to the successes that ensued. With what the bank now called the "single source of truth," forecasting modules to determine labour demand, automated scheduling algorithms to optimize fit and dashboard reporting and analytics to improve visibility, the team could now identify changes that led to significant improvements in efficiency. The integrated scheduling system, part of the workforce management solution, optimized the workload fit by tightly coupling individual worker profiles (available hours, skills, etc.) with the work to be done, eliminating significant waste. The schedules guided staff to specific activities every time they checked in, even suggesting appropriate break times. The bank was able to immediately recover the 10 percent variance between payroll and actual work and ultimately optimized workforce effectiveness in their operations by an average of 30 percent. In areas where additional staff was needed, management now had the tools with which to justify the increases.

But more than just reducing costs, the bank applied Lean principles to be able to put the right people in the right places, and at the right times and doing the right things. As a result, customer satisfaction (and value) increased as well. For the bank, Lean just worked.

By translating Lean principles from the original manufacturing lexicon to the back office, banks can create a powerful infrastructure to identify waste where it exists and to quantify the cost of doing business.

The three critical components of a Lean production program are; a program office that can train and deploy Lean practices across the enterprise, the consolidated and consistent activity data, and an automated scheduling solution that leverages that data. Activity-Based Costing is an important first step without the "single source of truth," improvements can't be made with any certainty as to the outcome. Ultimately, Lean production leads to a win-win-win situation, with the consumer reaping a higher-quality product, the bank staff benefiting from higher performance and more objective appraisals, and the bank itself performing better and producing (or servicing) at a lower cost.

Chapter 19: Lean Banking Success Stories

A number of financial institutions have employed lean in the manner we describe in this book and achieved impressive results. One major U.S. based global asset manager used it to redesign its core back-office processes, targeting both a significant increase in productivity and a revitalized, improvement-focused culture. The institution initiated the effort with a 12 week pilot focused on the securities-pricing process and it conducted workshops utilizing value-stream mapping and other lean tools to engage frontline workers and managers and solicit their ideas on how the process could be improved.

These workshops generated a range of actionable ideas that were subsequently developed further and validated. For example, the institution identified and eliminated multiple redundant verifications of individual equity prices throughout the value chain. Employees did not realize that they had all been performing those checks against the same reference data nor were they aware of the rigorous validation process performed by the centralized pricing group before the prices were sent out in the first place. The institution conducted similar workshops for frontline managers, which led to additional ideas that could be implemented broadly across the organization.

Throughout the pilot, and as the transformation was extended to other processes, the institution focused not just on the mechanics of process improvement but also on related organizational issues such as training, coaching, mentorship, and work allocation. It also instituted rigorous governance and change-management programs to sustain momentum.

As a result of these efforts, the institution was able to achieve reductions of approximately 20 percent in the number of full-time employees needed to fulfil the targeted processes. It also significantly reduced the probability of errors and achieved greater client satisfaction. Employee engagement and satisfaction also rose significantly, which, in turn, enhanced the institution's ability to broaden the overall lean transformation program.

A leading North American bank seeking overall process improvement launched a similar initiative and had comparable success. The bank initiated the effort with simultaneous eight-week pilots focused on its retail-mortgage and commercial-lending processes. It examined the processes end to end, working backward from the customer. It employed lean tools to engage management and frontline staff and to solicit, vet, and validate ideas for improvement. It placed a heavy emphasis on change management to ensure that the necessary cultural changes were initiated and reinforced.

The result; the bank significantly reduced cycle times and cost and improved quality. It also identified opportunities to realize significant longer-term gains in efficiency, including reductions of roughly 40 percent in processing time and 60 percent in total lead time in its retail-mortgage process and even larger gains in those areas in its commercial-lending process. The bank also gained confidence in its ability to execute additional lean transformations.

A global corporate and investment bank achieved similar gains through its deployment of lean. Through a series of mini-transformations over a period of 16 months, the bank made significant improvements in its credit-approval processes, whose operations spanned nearly 30 countries. The improvements occurred across three categories; process efficiency, the operating model, and employee behaviours. The bank's credit file, for example, was significantly simplified and standardized, and the application process was redesigned to take into account different clients and credit types. Measurable improvements included a 30 to 50 percent reduction in response time, a 15 to 30 percent boost in the productivity of credit analysts, and a freeing up of roughly 20 percent of relationship managers' time.

Lean can be a truly transformational tool for banks, one that delivers a step change in process efficiencies and builds a foundation for ongoing, organization-wide improvement. The key is to approach and implement it correctly. A holistic, end-to-end approach that is phased in incrementally and that effectively engages the frontline staff will realize all of lean's potential and ensure that the gains last.

Chapter 20: Bank Turns to Lean

What do you do when your business processes slow down to the point that your customers threaten to take their millions of dollars of business elsewhere?

When it happened to one of the world's largest banks, its leadership turned to Lean to set things right.

Surprised? If there is a general misconception about Lean, it's that its place is in manufacturing, not in service-oriented industries; but that is a fallacy. Industries like banking are starting to adopt Lean to transform their operations and become more efficient and customer-centric.

One of the primary goals of any service industry organization is, of course, to satisfy the customer. Like manufacturing companies, service providers rely on defined operating processes. Inefficient processes slow down transactions, and that frustrates customers.

In the case of the international bank, the initial problem was identified as the slow processing of customer documentary credit, known as "DC." The bank had begun experiencing a high number of DC escalation calls about 180 per week and operations personnel were swamped trying to solve customer issues. That, in turn, slowed down the normal process of trade service operations.
Concerned, the bank conducted a survey that found 80 percent of its customers felt that taking more than

two days to process DC was unacceptable. The survey results also showed that if the bank could cut the DC process to a day or less, customer satisfaction would increase from 58 percent to 71 percent.

Where do inefficient processes come from? In a global survey of senior executives that was conducted by The Economist, we found that many organizations have processes designed by circumstance, such as a merger, an acquisition, or tactical decisions made over a period of years. Other companies in the survey had processes designed by purpose, where issues were targeted and addressed within their value stream.

Organizations with "designed by circumstance" processes are destined to make repeated fixes to the same problems. Moreover, the survey showed they financially under-perform their peers. In contrast, companies with "designed by purpose" processes have a "fix it once" orientation, and in the survey they financially out-performed their peers.

So where does the journey start on the road to a "designed by purpose" 21st Century operating model? It starts with Lean.

"Designed by Purpose" Banking Processes

Long popular as the basis for avoiding waste and enhancing operating efficiencies, Lean is more of a philosophy than a collection of tools; but firms that intelligently embrace both the philosophy and the tools can gain considerable advantages. Lean can not only help expedite the processes that ensure customer satisfaction, it can turn around the entire flow of operations to improve business performance and reduce operations cost.

For the international bank in our example, the journey to Lean began with the formation of an internal Centre for Excellence team and the embrace of its Lean "surround methodology," a process utilizing case studies and train-the-trainer techniques to facilitate knowledge transfer and improve the organization's internal ability to solve process-related problems.

When you talk about DC and similar banking transactions, you are primarily talking about processes. So, what the bank did first was redesign the processes for all of the required steps of its DC transactions. Key questions were asked; Is this done the right way? What waste can we take out of the process? Why do you do that task that way? Are there steps that can be performed better?

Through a series of workshops, the bank and its consulting partner got deep into detail and designed a set of "processes with a purpose" around the theories of constraint and Lean tenets. Driving the design of these processes with intent, not circumstance, and leveraging Lean techniques forced the business to become customer-driven rather than internally-driven and note that change here wasn't about big technology spending. Instead, it involved rethinking the business through its processes as a way to address customer needs by eliminating wasted effort.

For example, in the course of issuing a DC, about a third of the time the bank's staff determined what clauses, or instructions, the customer wanted through a kind of "hunt-and-peck" process, such as looking at what the customer mentioned in their own format and converting them into the bank's standard format, or by looking up the customer's past preferences. This "designed by circumstance" process was slow and prone to error. Designing a process that required the desired clauses to be identified upfront by the customer eliminated the waste and accelerated the process.

Through a series of granular workshops based on Lean thinking, each inefficient and wasteful process was uncovered, discussed, and evaluated. Essential efficient processes were retained and others were streamlined or dropped.

Ultimately, this granular grassroots approach yielded information showing that the delays were also due to a number of seemingly unrelated factors, including a long wait time for application processing, an overly complicated application form that required redundant data, application batching, application errors, processing errors, and queuing issues.

Lean techniques kicked in to resolve these issues as well, with the bank and its consulting partner creating a single-piece process flow and layout changes to facilitate that single-piece flow. Then the proper control mechanisms were established to sustain the improvements over time.

A Phased Transformation

If all of this sounds simple and direct, it wasn't. The transformation purposely was conducted in five phases over more than two years. That is because the phased approach allowed step-by-step transformations to take place so that the bank's staff could reap benefits at the end of each phase; and reaped benefits translated into increased confidence as the team entered the next phase of the transformation.

The first phase started by addressing the issue of change management itself, since the bank's process owners were reluctant to buy into the idea of implementing what they perceived to be manufacturing-oriented concepts. This is where the workshops with relevant case studies played a key role by showcasing relevant business success stories.

Since the "surround methodology" of the transformation initiative involved an organizational culture shift, awareness programs for the bank's employees were held to communicate the expected benefits to the business and the employees. The bank's consulting partner created an ownership mentality in the organization by identifying change agents and designating them as project leaders. Then they were trained on the methodology and on facilitation skills, train-the-trainer capabilities and project management. Significantly, the outcomes of the project were positioned as solutions generated by the bank's team, not by the consultants.

The initial results of the transformation included a 65 percent improvement in turnaround time and a financial saving to the bank of close to half a million dollars annually. But the subsequent results were even better. Following the transformation, the bank improved same-day DC turnaround from 20 percent to 90 percent, quadrupled its business capacity, and saved several million dollars annually in operating cost.

Ultimately, the transformation went beyond DC issuance to cut across all international trade products and services.

Lean Takeaways for Banking

For banks and other service organizations looking to Lean to improve customer-oriented processes, consider these three takeaways from our example:

1. Total transformation takes time, and patience is required to reap the largest and most important organizational benefits. The best approach is a phased transformation over a period of time.

2. In generating ideas for process improvements, involving and probing the process stakeholders in a grassroots approach is invaluable so that they own the ideas and are more inclined to adopt them. The large concept approach may not touch on key issues and could create resistance among staff.

3. Create a culture of success and a "design by purpose" approach to processing issues by creating a foundation in which change through Lean is embraced and builds on itself. You will find that the initial grassroots team will buy into both the approach and the Lean concepts as part of its ongoing operations, creating new success stories to pass along in subsequent transformation phases and initiatives.

While Lean is based on an engineering approach, it can be applied flexibly in the service arena where people, not machines, are critical to success. Success requires a balancing act between implementing the most optimal theoretical approaches and implementing what is humanly practical in problem-solving. Once employees see the true benefits of design by purpose they will embrace it, customers will reward it, and everyone will benefit.

Chapter 21: Conclusion

Banking Sector have through unexpected change over the past decade as they have redirected their attention from products to customers, developed new consumer friendly channels, and underwent numerous mergers. The outcome of these changes was the adoption of extremely complicated business models and systems that seem to impede cost reduction.

On the other side, the impressive achievements in manufacturing productivity and effectiveness have been the results of a long process of improvement through the application of scientific management methods collectively termed as "Lean Manufacturing" or "Toyota Production System". Unfortunately, these achievements have yet to affect business practices in the service sector, but as western economies are becoming more service-oriented, in order to maintain and advance their competitiveness, they focus considerable attention on cost effectiveness, quality excellence, and responsiveness.

All these aspects are directly related to lean principles, which are beginning to attract considerable attention in th service sector. The goal of this book was to investigate and educate our readers on the applicability of Lean Manufacturing Principles in banking environments and to derive guidelines for the transformation of these principles in banks.

As in all service businesses, the aim in banking is to increase both speed and quality at all levels. To deliver bank services more quickly is an essential element for the bank to become more flexible and to better respond to changing customer demands and market conditions. Faster services are delivered by fewer hands and by eliminating unnecessary steps. For example when processing payment orders faster, the bank reduces opportunity costs and customers are more satisfied.

To focus simultaneously on quality means to establish specifications and collect metrics, applying tools to reduce variance, prevent failures and attack root cause.

Both strategies (focus on speed and focus on quality) have as consequences lowering costs, cement customer loyalty by offering higher quality service and increasing revenues.

In banking (especially in Retail Banking), variety increases complexity and should be vigilantly examined and reduced whenever possible. Any increase in complexity directly increases the risk of both slower and defective services, and increase support and maintenance costs in the form of overtaxed back-office processing procedures, too many customer-service systems and too much staff training.

Card issuer Credit Europe Bank is an example of service organization that separates common services from unique services and it gains value from each.

Another Lean Management approach that has been developed in banking is to enable frontline staff to engage customers more independently with less management oversight. In this way the frontline staff will operate, instead of having to seek approval for decisions.

This setup also frees staff from focusing on basic transactions and allows them to give more personal attention to customers and have a more direct impact on increasing revenue. For example, In some Banks when a customer has an issue, staff is both enabled and required to break away from regular duties and immediately address the customer concern.

Banks, when applying Lean Management, should do the following:

1. Explicitly map the value stream to understand precisely what is required to complete the process task for the customer. The map will be used to continually eliminating wasteful practices.

2. Move beyond the misconception that transactions are not like products and design, source, assemble and deliver transactions.

3. Regularly use KAIZEN (incremental continuous improvement that increases the effectiveness of an activity to produce more value and less waste).

Lean Management is an embedded culture of understanding the customer's needs and requirements, while continuously striving to reduce waste and optimizing the performances of process people and infrastructure.

At all levels of the organization there must be a strong desire to evolve and be better. Lean Management must be applied from the top to the bottom of the organizational pyramid.

In banking, by implementing Lean Management, the organization improves business performance using simple, practical tools and techniques to enhance quality, cost, delivery and people contribution.

Employees are not expected to simply routinely do their job, but are expected to contribute to the improvement of processes and operations, utilizing their own personal experience and creativity.

Good Luck!!

www.ingramcontent.com/pod-product-compliance
Lightning Source LLC
Chambersburg PA
CBHW051546170526
45165CB00002B/907